Come Out To Play

Mary Witt

A Samuel French Acting Edition

SAMUEL FRENCH

FOUNDED 1830

SAMUELFRENCH-LONDON.CO.UK
SAMUELFRENCH.COM

CHARACTERS

Aunt Helen, a spinster in her late thirties
Emily Davenport, her young ward
Connie Clayton, a musical-comedy actress
Agatha, the housemaid
Cook

The action takes place in Aunt Helen's drawing-room

Time – the Edwardian era

COME OUT TO PLAY

A drawing-room in Edwardian times

The furniture is tall and uncluttered. There is a screen of William Morris design, a desk with a chair, a settee, an occasional chair, a pie-crust table, and a tall palm on a delicate wooden stand. There is a small handbell on the table. Near the desk is a wrought iron lamp-stand. Colours are muted

As the Curtain rises, Aunt Helen is discovered seated at the desk, writing, with her back to Emily who is sitting on the settee with a number of papers. Aunt Helen, a spinster in her late thirties, wears a dress of grey or lavender, with lace at the high neck and wrists— it touches the floor and has a slight train. She walks without lifting her skirt. Emily Davenport, her young ward, wears a white muslin flapper dress, with sash, black stockings and shoes. She has long hair with a very large black bow at the back

Throughout the following scene there is an air of earnestness and seriousness

Emily Aunt Helen.

Aunt Helen makes no reply

Aunt Helen!
Aunt Helen (*without raising her head from writing*) Yes, Emily?
Emily I have finished the list of Committees you asked me to compile. I find that you are on thirty-two of them and I am on sixteen.
Aunt Helen Excellent, Emily. You are doing very well. I feel that between us we shall be able to do a great deal of good.
Emily Oh, do you really think so? (*She rises and takes the list over to Aunt Helen, who looks down it carefully*)
Aunt Helen Certainly. We have a duty to show the lower classes that life is earnest, and meant for hard work, not careless, thoughtless enjoyment.
Emily (*obediently*) Yes, Aunt.

Aunt Helen Now, let me see. I was especially pleased to be elected Chairman of the Rights of Women Campaign. You have that down here somewhere, I hope?

Emily Yes, Aunt. (*Pointing*) At the bottom of the page.

Aunt Helen I did, however, mention to the Committee that I should prefer not to take part in public meetings of this particular campaign. The previous Chairman was bodily assaulted by an angry husband, and by the time she had turned to face him he had disappeared into the crowd.

Emily How disgraceful!

Aunt Helen I should not wish to be exposed to such an indignity.

Emily (*referring to the list in her aunt's hand*) A problem has arisen in connection with the Sale of Work on behalf of the natives of Bangoola.

Aunt Helen Oh dear! Not another one!

Emily I'm afraid so. The largest contribution of articles for the sale was to be by the Ladies' Work Society, and unfortunately every one of its members made the same embroidered tea-cosy.

Aunt Helen How very odd! However did that happen?

Emily There was a very elegant pattern for one in last month's edition of the *Lady's Realm* magazine, and presumably they *all* found it irresistible.

Aunt Helen We really cannot have a stall filled with dozens of the same kind of cosy. I wonder if the cosies could be used by the natives as some kind of garment. Headgear, perhaps? We must see what the Committee say. I hope they will not spend too much time arguing over it. There are occasions when they are more of a hindrance than a help.

Emily I suppose we must have Committees?

Aunt Emily Oh, certainly we must. They afford us the support of respectable names, and the lady with money but no breeding will gladly contribute to any cause which enables her to sit next to the lady with breeding but no money.

Emily (*sighing*) I don't suppose I shall ever be able to manage a Committee as well as you do.

Aunt Helen (*briskly*) Of course you will, my dear. You have great promise, and I have faith in you. Simply ensure that your stays are comfortable, that your back hair is not in danger of collapse, remain cool at all times, and you cannot fail. In fact, on the one occasion when I have seen you in the chair, I felt I could not have done better myself.

Emily How very kind of you, Aunt Helen!

Aunt Helen Not at all, child. Now, what have we next? Ah, the Bazaar for Ladies in Distressed Circumstances. I should like to have a plan to put before the Committee myself, otherwise they will all put forward their own, which are frequently quite impossible.

Emily Who shall we ask to open the Bazaar?

Aunt Helen Yes, that is a most important point. We have had the Royal Princesses rather often, and they do not seem to have very much money. We need someone who will be eager to come before the public, and willing to spend freely for the privilege. An entertainer, perhaps?

Emily Could we ask Daisy Duveen, the actress? The public are *very* interested in her, as she is said to be a favourite of His Majesty, though not *quite* so popular with the dear Queen . . .

The door opens and Agatha, the housemaid, appears, visible only from the waist downwards. Above, she is shrouded by an enormous basket of flowers

Aunt Helen Agatha! What is this!

Agatha's flushed face appears round the side of the basket

Agatha It's a basket of flahs, m'm. It's come from next door. Mr Jarvis's boot-boy just brung it, with Mr Jarvis's compliments. The flahs are all from his garding, and he says if you've any occasion to go out today, his carriage is at your disposal.

Aunt Helen (*astonished, but controlling herself*) Put the basket down, Agatha. That is all, thank you.

Agatha goes

(*Letting her annoyance show*) What effrontery! What can be the matter with the creature next door, and what will the servants think? He has been in that house for less than a month, and without waiting for our cards to be left on him, presumes to strike up an acquaintance.

Emily (*examining the basket*) He has undoubtedly cut off the largest and choicest blooms for your benefit.

Aunt Helen (*tapping her foot*) Then he has made the sacrifice in vain, since I have no intention whatever of calling upon him. And in any case, what can be his object?

Emily (*thoughtfully*) I have noticed that he watches from his window when you go to meetings.

Aunt Helen How ridiculous!

Emily And though I thought nothing of it at the time, he has been, one might almost say—lurking—in his front garden, perhaps to catch your attention.

Aunt Helen But why? He cannot surely be interested in the Campaign for the Rights of Women.

Emily No, it is more likely to be the Rights of Man, for I believe, Aunt Helen, that he is in love with you.

Aunt Helen (*reacting*) In love with me? Such an idea is utterly preposterous! *Utterly!* We must put an end to this impossible situation without delay. I will send a note to this Mr *Jarvis*— (*contemptuously*)—and ask him to call on me this afternoon. I fancy I shall be able to make him see how disagreeable both he and his intentions are. Please ring for Agatha.

Emily rings the bell on the small table. Aunt Helen sits at the desk and vigorously dashes off a note, puts it in an envelope, and seals it

Agatha enters, and waits until the letter is ready

Will you please see that this basket is conveyed immediately to the Cottage Hospital, and explain that it is a gift from Mr Jarvis.

Agatha (*mystified*) Yes, m'm.

Aunt Helen And would you yourself take this note next door to Mr Jarvis at once, please. (*She hands Agatha the note*)

Agatha Yes, m'm.

Agatha picks up the basket and staggers out

Aunt Helen (*triumphantly*) I shall enjoy telling Mr Jarvis exactly what we in this household feel about male domination in general, and about his efforts to ingratiate himself with me in particular. (*She resumes her writing*)

Emily sits on the settee and examines papers

Emily (*after a pause*) Aunt Helen. (*Pause*) Aunt Helen!
Aunt Helen Yes?
Emily Yesterday, when I was helping at the Sale of Work, I overheard a conversation between Mrs Prendergast and Mrs Beecham . . . (*She trails off*)
Aunt Helen (*with some contempt*) Those two ladies regard a Sale of Work as an opportunity provided solely for them to exchange gossip. You may safely disregard anything they say.
Emily Yes, but—they were talking about me and about father.

Aunt Helen does not turn round, but her back stiffens and shows that she is tense

Aunt Helen (*quietly*) What did they say?
Emily Mrs Prendergast said to Mrs Beecham—they did not know I was behind some potted palms arranging the fancy stall—"I shall never understand how Colonel Davenport, or 'Handsome Jack', as we called him, came to have such a goody-goody daughter as Emily." (*She stands and walks slowly round the settee, then leans on the back and looks down at her clasped hands, which are twisting together*)
Aunt Helen (*turning in her chair*) Yes?
Emily And then Mrs Beecham said, "You need not look farther than her 'Aunt Helen'." What did she mean?
Aunt Helen Whatever doubts may have been planted in your mind, Emily, may be absolutely dismissed. (*Grimly*) It is obvious that I must have a little talk with these two ladies. Not only shall I make it clear how harmful such gossip is, but I shall also point out one or two small items in their own lives that they would not be at all anxious to have revealed. Your father was a man of the highest—the *very* highest principles, and I know that he would be proud to see the work that you are doing. I hope that your one aim in life will be to earn the approval which I am sure he would have given.
Emily (*mechanically*) Yes, Aunt Helen.
Aunt Helen Just before he died he chose my mother to look after you, because she had always been a mother to him. And when she died, the task of bringing you up became mine. From the beginning, young as I was, I felt it my duty to guide you on the paths of high moral conduct, along which my mother had always guided me, and to protect you from the perils of

frivolity and selfish pleasure-seeking which surround us on all sides. I have never spared myself in carrying out that duty, Emily, and I have always endeavoured, by my own way of life, to set you a clear and inspiring example of dedication and service to the lower orders.

Emily I shall always be grateful to you, Aunt Helen.

Aunt Helen (*businesslike once more*) Now it is time for my afternoon rest. I shall leave you to continue with your work whilst I go and lie down.

Aunt Helen goes out

Emily sits on the settee and becomes absorbed in her papers

Agatha's head appears round the door. She looks cautiously round the room, then puts two fingers in her mouth and whistles to attract Emily's attention

Agatha I've took the letter, Miss Emily, and I've been to the library and got you a new book. (*She holds up a library book*)

Emily springs up, gay and excited—though cautious in case Aunt Helen should be near: she appears full of life and rather mischievous

Emily Oh Agatha! You are a dear! What is it?

Agatha It's your favourite, Miss Emily. Guess who!

Emily Agatha! Is it—can it be—Miss Marie Corelli?

Agatha (*delighted at her success*) Yes, it is, miss. I seed a lady in front of me at the library with a little dog under her arm. She was changing her book and she dropped it. So I picked it up, very polite, and seed who it was by. So I asked for it and the man behind the counter give it to me. "Is it good?" I says, and he says, "It's the latest!"

Emily (*thrilled*) What is it called?

Agatha (*reading the title*) It's called *Sundered Hearts.*

Emily (*disappointed*) Surely we had that last week?

Agatha No, miss. That was—(*very clearly*)—*Hearts Asunder.* You remember—where the heroine was very cold and'aughty and she's secretly pining for the 'ero and he goes off into the jungle and she says she's going to follow 'im barefoot to the

ends of the earth . . . (*She takes a breath*) *You* remember,
miss.

Emily (*ecstatically*) Oh yes, Agatha. Wasn't it *lovely*! Oh, it was
so romantic!

*They both stand for a moment lost in a dream of romance. A distant
bell rings*

Agatha Oh, there's the door-bell, Miss Emily. I must fly. But
Cook says would you be so kind as to let her have a read of the
book when you've finished it.

Emily Yes, of course I will. (*She hastily tucks the book under the
settee cushions*) I wonder who our visitor is. Unless it is a close
friend, Agatha, you had better say we are not at home this
afternoon.

Agatha (*suddenly the conventional servant again*) Yes, miss.

Agatha goes

*Emily sits on the settee and withdraws the book from under the
cushion. She dips into it with great relish for a moment or two, until
the door opens. She hastily pushes it back under the cushion*

Agatha enters, rather agitated

Agatha It's a lady, Miss Emily, and she wouldn't take Not At
Home for an answer.

*Connie Clayton enters. She is strikingly dressed, with feather boa,
gloves and handbag, and has a definite stage presence. She takes
off the gloves and feather boa, standing easily and looking all
round the room. In spite of Agatha's attempts to take them, she
tosses gloves and boa on to a chair with a careless gesture*

*Emily rises as Connie enters, and stands uncertainly, not knowing
quite what to do*

Connie You must be Emily. (*She smiles*) Emily Davenport.

Emily Yes, I am afraid I . . .

Connie I am Connie Clayton. (*She waits for a reaction*)

Agatha (*in the background*) Connie Clayton! (*She puts her hand
to her mouth*)

Emily (*primly*) Good afternoon, Miss Clayton. Are you perhaps from the Society for the Diffusion of Useful Knowledge?

Connie (*easily*) Well, I'm not actually a member, but I think you could say I have its interests at heart. I see you have never heard of me.

Emily (*seeing Agatha's round eyes*) Thank you, Agatha. You may go.

Agatha goes, walking backwards, staring at Connie until she has reached the door, when she turns and runs

Emily (*starting again with great politeness*) Have you come to see Aunt Helen?

Connie Not exactly. It was you I really wanted to see.

Emily Oh. Well, won't you sit down?

They sit together on the settee. Connie takes Emily's hand, in spite of the latter's slight withdrawal at this familiarity

Connie Many years ago, Emily, your father and I were friends—great friends . . .

Emily (*thrilled*) How wonderful! Do you not feel a better woman for having known him? Aunt Helen has told me so often of his highminded principles, his stern determination to improve the morals of those around him and his constant fight to check foolish frivolity and pleasure!

Connie (*looking at her oddly*) Aunt Helen has told you all this?

Emily Many, many times. It is the knowledge of such an example that enables us to carry on with our arduous social work.

Connie (*interested*) What social work do you do?

Emily (*collecting up the list of Committees*) We both serve on a great number of Committees. There, you see!

Connie (*scanning the list*) Heavens above! This must leave you very little time for going out with young men.

Emily Aunt Helen says we must restrict our acquaintanceship with the opposite sex to those who have reached the age when they are only interested in women's minds, not their bodies.

Connie (*drily*) They must be rather scarce. Don't you ever get taken to the theatre or to a ball?

Emily (*a little sadly*) Father would not have wished it. And in any case, Aunt Helen says that the animal nature of man makes him of no use whatever in women's struggle for emancipation.

Connie Oh dear!

Emily (*loftily*) Aunt Helen says——

Connie I think I've got a fairly good idea of what Aunt Helen says. I shall look forward to our meeting again.

Emily She is having her afternoon's rest at the moment, and will not care to be disturbed. Were you a great friend of hers, too?

Connie I knew her well in the old days, long before you came on the scene. I went to India before your father married, and there I have been ever since. But now I am back I wanted so much to see you. You're awfully like your father, you know.

Emily (*eagerly*) Tell me where you first saw him.

Connie Do you really want to know?

Emily Oh yes, yes!

Connie Well then, it was . . . (*She rises, as if naturally to take the centre of the floor*)

Cook appears in the doorway, leaning against it, one hand on her bosom, panting heavily through having hurried up the stairs. For a few seconds she cannot speak, staring at Connie. Then she moves to her and puts both hands on either side of her face and kisses her

Emily sits, thunderstruck

Agatha appears in the doorway, goggling, her apron to her mouth

Cook It is you—our very own Connie Clayton, the Norwich Nightingale! Will I ever forget you! I thought we would never see you again, my dear, dear soul!

Connie (*laughing and hugging Cook, in affectionate mockery*) Dear, dear Ethel!

Emily watches in staggered astonishment

You were the best dresser and wardrobe-mistress in the business. What are you doing here, and why did you leave the old Gaiety?

Cook (*wiping her eyes*) Why, Miss Connie, it seemed like after
you got married so grand and went out to India, that things
were never the same again. I hung on for a bit, until I heard
that Colonel Davenport, your old sweetheart, that's Emily's
father as was—(*completely oblivious of Emily's dazed look*)—
had to come back from Africa with a babe in arms, poor
widowed man. And we remembered how we'd thought, miss,
begging your pardon, as how you two might make a match of
it some day—

Connie turns her face away and plays with a brooch at her neck

—and he took me on, I reckon to remember you, and I took
him on for the self same reason. And I made up my mind that
wherever his little Emily was I would go, so here I am, as
Cook! (*She wipes her eyes again*)
Emily (*to Connie, faintly*) Does this mean you were in the
theatre?
Connie (*giving a low and splendidly graceful curtsey*) Yes, Emily,
indeed it does! I was one of the Gaiety Girls!
Agatha (*moving into the room slightly*) Oo! Miss—a real live Gaiety
Girl!
Emily I have heard Aunt Helen mention them. Can they truly
have been so abandoned?
Connie Abandoned? Oh my goodness, my dear Emily, the Gaiety
Girls were an absolute model of ladylike virtue. Dear old
George Edwardes saw to that. Mind you, we were the *crème
de la crème* at the Gaiety Theatre. We didn't *do* anything.
There were always eight of us, standing at the back of the
theatre—(*she stands in a sideways attitude, face turned to the
audience with a bright smile, holding an imaginary parasol as a
stick*)—wearing the most *divine* clothes, yards of lace and
chiffon, acres of beads and tassels.

*Emily gradually becomes entranced by the picture presented, and
reclines on the settee with her chin on her hands and her elbows on
the arm*

Cook (*with a chuckle, leaning relaxed on the back of a chair*) It
gave me a headache looking after 'em, I can tell you!
Connie (*clasping her hands in ecstasy*) Oh! The queues of young

men waiting outside the stage door for us—all with flowers and chocolates and invitations to supper! But we had to behave with absolute proprietary—George Edwardes said that if we did we should all become duchesses.

Emily (*breathlessly*) And did you?

Connie Some of us did, and we all married well, and for love, too. You can marry a rich man for love, you know, as well as a poor one.

Emily And who did you marry?

Connie (*smiling reminiscently*) Ah! He was the world's darling. Such a funny little man—he could never believe that anyone would want to marry him except for his money, and he had lots of that.

Cook I remember the night he proposed, Miss Connie, right after the third act, and there was I hanging up your costumes, out of sight behind the screen, and trapped, and not daring to come out! (*She laughs heartily, then sighs*)

Connie (*smiling a little sadly*) He came in carrying a beautiful ermine cloak as a present for me, and he put it down on the floor and knelt on it, and said, "I know nobody could really want to have me, but will you marry me?" And I did so want loving just then—

Cook (*sagely*) Because you'd just had a big quarrel with Colonel Davenport and he'd gone off in a huff.

Connie —so I said "Yes", and I've never regretted it.

Emily Then you might have married my father!

Connie Perhaps.

Emily And then you would have been my mother! (*She seems about to become emotional*)

Cook (*to Connie, hastily*) And do you remember old Sam, at the Stage Door? He used to keep out the Stage Door Johnnies who meant no good to the young 'uns in the chorus.

Connie Dear old Sam.

Cook (*vigorously*) You're the only one who thought so, Miss Connie. I reckon you could see an angel where the rest of us only saw an old skinflint. We know you helped him when he needed money, like you helped lots of others, and I don't know how it was, after you left he seemed to shrivel, somehow, and never spoke to no-one. Then he died, and that's more'n twenty years ago now.

Connie Twenty years! And long before that I sang my first song. (*Dreamily*) I can hear it now.

Slowly and reminiscently Connie sings two lines from a waltz song, Cook and Agatha joining in and swaying gently)

*"One more kiss, love, the morning is breaking—
    We have danced through the night—In a dream of romance..."
Cook How those audiences loved you! When you sang that, Colonel Davenport said you could see the old Gaiety swaying from side to side from the people singing with you. Those were wonderful days, and you were the most wonderful part of them to us. Weren't we thrilled when you got your first leading part in *The Toast of Vienna*. That hat you wore in it, like a great umbrella—everyone had to have a hat like it. (*With delighted laughter*) Do you remember the scene where you were pretending to be a French singer, and had to dance on the table. Then you took off your garter and threw it to the gentlemen in the front rows! My goodness, trying to get a seat in the front rows then was like trying to get into Buckingham Palace.

Agatha is now well into the room, all class distinctions forgotten. Cook is completely at home with her dear Miss Connie. Emily stands in thrilled silence

Connie (*laughing*) The first night I could hardly sing that song—I was shaking like a leaf!
Emily (*at last won over*) Oh, I would do love to have seen you!
Cook Go on, Miss Connie, let's hear you just once more.

Connie, laughing, takes on the role of a French girl, dancing lightly, and singing with a French accent

Connie (*singing*)
  *Zey say to me—Oh oh Delphine, and I say Oo la la!
   But when zey whisper in my ear, I cry 'You go too far!'
   I will not turn ze ozzer cheek so you can steal a kiss
   How dare you ask, you naughtee boys—But I will give you *ziss*!

As Connie sings, Aunt Helen appears unnoticed in the background

* *See page 20*

*At the end of the song, Connie whips up her front petticoats, show-
lots of lace and frills, slips off a garter and throws it into the air.
Agatha and cook clap, and Emily runs to catch it, but stops frozen
as Aunt Helen's voice is heard.*

Aunt Helen What is the meaning of this extraordinary scene?

*Cook and Agatha do not wait to be told, but exit unobtrusively,
though quite unintimidated*

Connie (*unperturbed*) Helen!
Aunt Helen (*with irony*) Connie! (*She comes forward to face
Connie so that they now occupy the centre of the room like
antagonists. Emily retreats behind the settee, bewildered at all that
has been happening*
Connie (*Brightly*) Well, Helen, you have—*hardly* changed at all
since I last saw you twenty years ago.
Aunt Helen I am gratified that you have called after such a long
time.
Connie India is rather a long way off for paying afternoon calls
in Kensington, but I would have tried to come before if I'd
known Emily was with you. Since my old darling died there
was nothing to keep me in India, so I came home. And the
first thing I made up my mind to do was to look up old friends,
and that's how I found out that there was a little Emily
Davenport. (*She smiles at Emily*)
Aunt Helen Emily and I are grateful for your interest, and I have
no doubt whatever that Emily has been able to draw her own
conclusions from the example of your talents that we have just
seen. (*Dismissingly*) And now, may I ask you to excuse us?
Connie (*forthrightly*) You certainly need an excuse of some sort.
What is all this nonsense you have been filling Emily's head
with?
Aunt Helen I have no idea what you mean.
Connie Oh yes, you have. When Emily's father gave her into
your mother's charge, he certainly didn't intend that she should
be brought up cut off from the world's enjoyments as if she
was in a nunnery. Jack—why he loved life more than anyone
I ever knew. All his days were full of laughter and friendship
and kindness. He made the world seem a brighter place, even
for the poor and unhappy . . .

Aunt Helen (*furiously*) You are trying to undo all my years of work and dedication . . .

Connie Dedication fiddlesticks! *You* are trying to turn Emily from a warm, loving human being into a cold statue like yourself. Why? Why have you made her believe that her father was someone so terrifyingly and inhumanly perfect? And quite impossible to live up to?

Emily Oh, Miss Clayton, was my father really not like that after all—so stern and puritanical?

Connie Of course he wasn't, my dear. He would have wanted you to live, not to dry and shrivel up into an old maid. He would have wanted you to make use of every moment. (*Gaily*) Where are all the young men who should be dancing with you, holding your flowers, fetching and carrying at your slightest wish, begging for one kiss . . .

Aunt Helen You are absolutely disgusting! How dare you put such ideas into an innocent girl's head! She has pledged herself to give her life to the poor and needy, to improve their lot.

Connie (*contemptuously*) She has pledged her life to a lot of old fogeys on committees, you mean. These poor people you talk about never see her except at a distance. What they want is human warmth and sympathy. You think if you give them an indoor bathroom they've nothing else to wish for. How wrong you are!

Aunt Helen (*showing anger*) This comes well from someone who exhibited herself before low audiences . . .

Connie Haven't you enough human feelings to realize that these low audiences, as you call them, were able to forget their troubles and sorrows in the romance and glitter of the theatre? To hear how they laughed and cheered up there in the gods— that was the supreme joy.

Emily (*to Aunt Helen*) Why did you deceive me about my father? All this time I could have been loving him instead of fearing him.

Aunt Helen All I have said is true, Emily. He was noble beyond all other men. No-one could ever reach the high pinnacle on which he stood . . .

Connie (*bursting out*) I see it all, now! You were in love with him! But you were only a child then, and you had no idea what love really meant. So you created an impossibly perfect image of him in your childish mind—a false image, which you and Emily have been worshipping all these years!

Connie is accusing and triumphant. There is an electric silence

Cook, oblivious of the atmosphere, appears in the doorway, dressed in outdoor clothes, with black bonnet and cape. She carries a suitcase to which an umbrella is strapped, and puts these down beside her

Cook (*with great determination*) Miss Helen, m'm. I'm giving in my notice. Now Miss Connie's come back there's only one place for me. Miss Connie, I couldn't rest happy away from you, and you knows it. So I'm being so bold as to take your consent to coming with you for granted. We've been through such happy times together, and I wouldn't want to be with anyone else but you, now you're back again. So I'll put my things in the cab as is waiting outside. Good-bye, Miss Helen. And good-bye, Miss Emily.

Cook goes, taking her baggage

Aunt Helen stands as if stunned

Connie (*to her*) I am going now, Helen. Please forgive Cook for leaving you—I have made up my mind to return to the theatre, and this is where we both belong.

Emily (*passionately*) Oh please, please let me come, too. I know that with you I could really live and laugh and be happy. And you could tell me everything you know about my dear, dear father. I feel as if I have been asleep and you have just come to waken me to life. Say I may come. (*She clings to Connie*) Say I may be free.

Connie It is for your Aunt Helen to say whether you shall or not. I shall not take you away without her consent. Good-bye, Helen. (*She moves to the door*) I shall be outside, Emily— waiting.

Connie exits

Emily (*anguished*) O please, Aunt Helen—tell me I may go with
   her.
Aunt Helen (*lifelessly, raising her head*) Very well, Emily. I shall
   not try to keep you here—you are free to go.

Emily runs to the door

   Emily . . .

Emily turns

   If you go with her—I shall be—(*she falters*)—quite alone.

Emily, though now eager to leave, turns back consolingly

   Oh no, Aunt, you will not be alone. You will have all your
   Committees, and your work for Women's Rights. There is so
   much to be done. (*Showing emotion*) I shan't forget you. (*She
   makes as if to come back and kiss Aunt Helen, then blows her
   a quick kiss and runs off*)

   Emily exits

*Aunt Helen stands quite still, as if stunned, one hand grasping the
back of a chair, her head bent*

   The door opens and Agatha peeps in

Agatha Mr Jarvis has arrived, Miss Helen. He says you asked
   him to call.
Aunt Helen (*with a sudden gesture*) Tell him I cannot . . . (*She
   stops suddenly*) No. (*She raises her head proudly*) Wait! I shall
   receive Mr Jarvis after all. Tell him I *am* at home, Agatha, and
   show him in.
Agatha Yes, m'm.

   Agatha curtsies and exits

*Aunt Helen stands thinking for a moment, then her eye falls on the
red garter. She looks at it fixedly, then suddenly and impulsively
bends swiftly down and picks it up, looking over her shoulder at the*

door as she does so. Then she lifts up her skirt, displaying lots of lace petticoat, raises her foot and slips the garter on to her leg below the knee. With a half-daring laugh, she stretches out her leg to admire it, and drops her skirts. Quickly, with a secret smile, she adjusts the lace at her neck and wrists, smooths her hands down over her bodice and skirt, and turns to face the door, standing in a seductive attitude

Agatha enters, standing to one side

Agatha Mr Jarvis to see you, ma'am.

CURTAIN

LIGHTING PLOT

Property fittings required: wrought-iron lamp standard (dressing only)
Interior. A drawing-room

To open: General daylight lighting

No cues

EFFECTS PLOT

Cue 1   **Emily:** "Oh, it was so romantic!"   (Page 7)
Distant door-bell rings

FURNITURE AND PROPERTY LIST

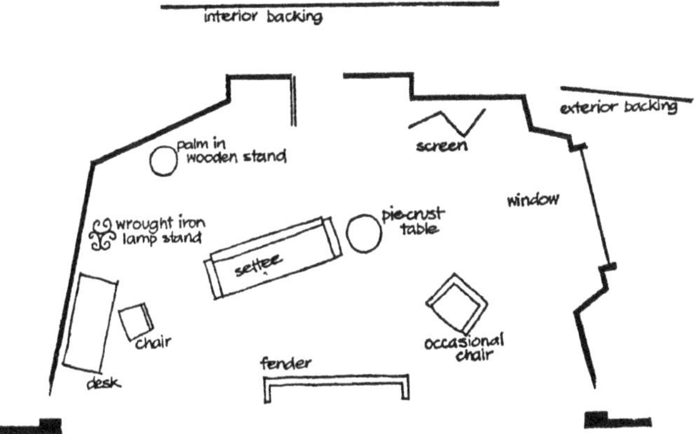

On stage: Settee. *On it:* cushions, various papers and folders
Desk chair
Occasional chair
Desk. *On it:* papers, writing materials, pens, notepaper, envelopes
Pie-crust table. *On it:* small handbell
Morris screen
Palm on wooden stand
Wrought-iron lamp standard
Fender and fire-irons
Carpet
Hearth-rug
Window curtains

Off stage: Large basket of flowers **(Agatha)**
Library book **(Agatha)**
Suitcase and umbrella **(Cook)**

Zey say to me Oh Oh Del-phine and I say O la la!
But when zey whis-per in my ear I cry you go too far
I will not turn ze oz-zer cheek so you can steal a kiss
Recitative
How dare you ask you naughty boys but I will give you ziss

Waltz
One more kiss love, the morn —— ing is break —— ing.
We have danced through the night in a dream of ro- mance